MEGATECH

Super Subs

Exploring the deep sea

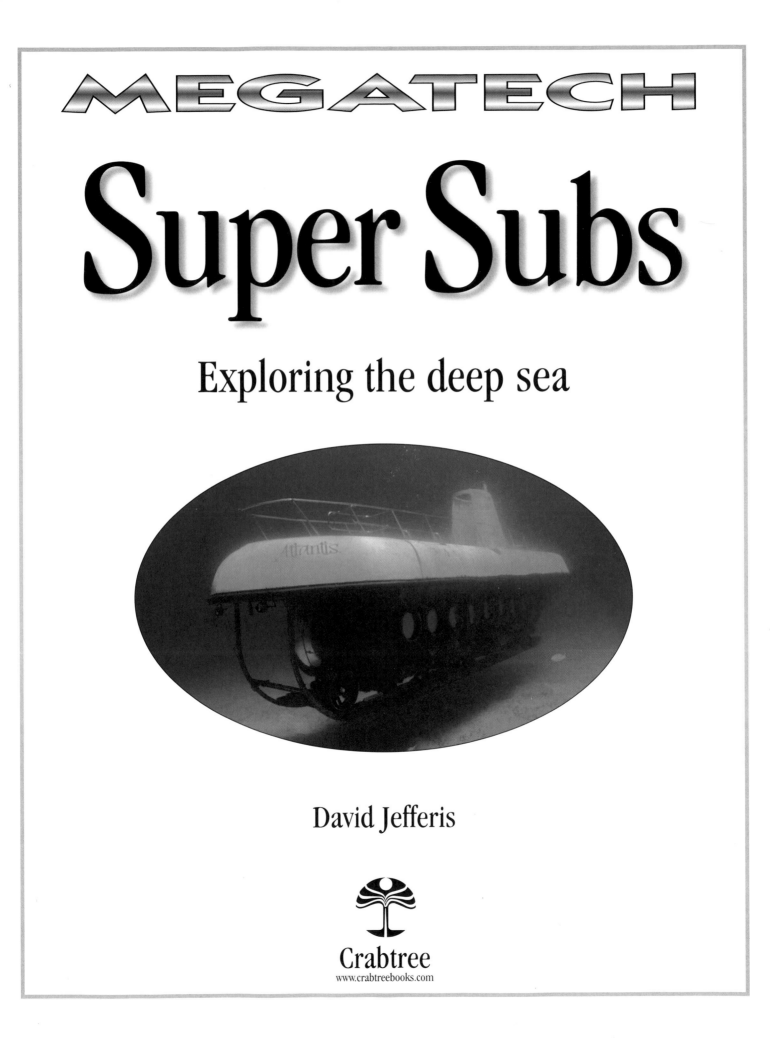

David Jefferis

Crabtree
www.crabtreebooks.com

Introduction

The deep sea has been called "inner space" because it is an unexplored region of the Earth for most of us. Yet, there are many people whose jobs take them far below the surface of the planet's oceans. About two million people a year also take trips in tourist submarines.

Most submarines are used by the world's navies. More than 700 submarines cruise below the waves. Ocean researchers also use both crewed subs and remote-operated vehicles, or **ROV**s, underwater. Completely automatic robotic subs are also being developed. These do not need humans to control their movements.

Will humans ever live in undersea cities, as some scientists used to think? It seems less likely today because ROVs and robotic subs can do much of the work of humans underwater. Scientists hope to use these super subs to collect such things as minerals and sea plants for use in industry and medicines.

Crabtree Publishing Company
PMB 16A,
350 Fifth Avenue
Suite 3308
New York
NY 10118

612 Welland Avenue
St Catharines
Ontario
L2M 5V6

Edited by
Isabella McIntyre
Coordinating editor
Ellen Rodger
Project editor
P.A. Finlay

Production coordinator
Rose Gowsell
Technical consultant
Mat Irvine FRBS

Picture research by
Kay Rowley

Created and produced by
Alpha Communications in association
with Firecrest Books Ltd.

©2002 David Jefferis/Alpha
Communications

Cataloging-in-Publication Data
Jefferis, David.
    Super Subs : opening up undersea
frontiers / David Jefferis.
    p. cm. -- (Megatech)
    Includes index.
    Summary: Describes different
types of submarine vehicles and their
development, discussing their various
uses for military purposes, undersea
exploration, and ocean research.
    ISBN 0-7787-0053-4 --
    ISBN 0-7787-0063 -1 (pbk.)
    1. Submarines (Ships)--Juvenile
literature. 2. Underwater exploration--
Juvenile literature. 3. Oceanography--
Research--Juvenile literature. 4.
Submersibles--Juvenile literature. [1.
Submarines (Ships) 2. Underwater
exploration.] I. Title. II. Series.
    V857 .J4423 2002
    623.8'205--dc21

                    2001047523
                    LC

Color separation by
Embassy Graphics Ltd.

Printed by
Worzalla Publishing Company

Pictures on these pages, clockwise from
far left:
1   A hunter-killer nuclear submarine
shows off smooth lines.
2   A research craft uses powerful lights
when submerged.
3   Undersea life on a coral reef.
4   A submarine prepares to dive
after a mid-ocean linkup with a
surface ship.
5   Command crew on a nuclear
sub's fin, or conning tower.
6   Camera-equipped sub with
plastic bubble for good crew vision.

Previous page shows:
Atlantis sub takes tourists on an
adventure trip in the Bahamas.

Contents

World under the sea Our world is mostly water   4

SUBMARINES

Deep divers How a submarine works   6

Subs at war Deadly weapons beneath the sea   8

Nuclear submarine An important naval craft   10

Subs today Quiet, fast, and heavily armed   12

Sub hunters Deadly game of underwater cat and mouse   14

Rescue mission Helping a sub crew trapped on the seabed   16

UNDERSEA RESEARCH

Voyage to the deep Journey to the bottom of the sea   18

Finding wrecks Exploring sunken ships   20

Underwater workers Deep divers and their equipment   22

Oceans in peril? Managing the resources of the seas   24

SUMMARY

What's next? Possibilities for the near future   26

REFERENCE SECTION

Time track Submarine progress   28

Glossary Terms and concepts   30

Index   32

World under the sea

▲ *A military submarine stays on the surface while leaving port. Once on patrol, subs like this cruise underwater as quietly as possible, to stay hidden from enemies.*

P lanet Earth could really be called Ocean World because most of its surface is covered in water. From inland lakes and rivers to polar ice caps and oceans, 70 percent of Earth's surface is water.

Ice around the North Pole floats on open water

Strange animals live on the ocean bottoms

Pale blue areas are shallower than the deep oceans

Most of our planet's surface is covered in water. The three major oceans, the Pacific, Atlantic, and Indian, are interconnected. There is water under the floating ice of the North Pole area as well. Submarines can cruise anywhere there is enough water, even under the ice around the North Pole.

▶ *Over 70 percent of our planet's surface is covered in water. Shallow waters surround the continents and are called* continental shelves. *These are shown in pale blue. Deeper waters are colored dark blue.*

S ubmarines have a smooth-shaped body, or **hull**, and are designed to move underwater. Most subs are navy craft, equipped with **torpedoes** and missiles. **Submersibles** are smaller, and are often used for research or for tasks such as checking pipelines below the sea.

◀ *An undersea shark hunt, as imagined by an artist in 1883.*

The southern half of Earth is mostly ocean. Antarctica is a large, frozen continent that surrounds the South Pole.

The Pacific Ocean is the largest and deepest ocean

▲ *The* Alvin *is a three-person craft used by U.S. researchers. Its most famous trip was in 1985, to visit the wreck of the ocean ship* Titanic, *which sank in the Atlantic Ocean.*

In some parts of Antarctica, the ice is several miles thick

Only research subs can go down to the ocean floors. Military subs stay closer to the surface

Submersibles such as the *Alvin* tackle a wide variety of jobs. In the 1960s, the *Alvin* helped recover deadly bombs from a jet that had crashed into the Mediterranean Sea. In the 1980s, the *Alvin* was in the Atlantic Ocean, searching for the *Titanic*, a passenger ship that sank in 1912, after hitting an iceberg. Today, the *Alvin* is still used regularly for research.

How deep are the oceans?

The average depth of all the oceans is about 12,000 ft (3700 m). Surrounding the continents are much shallower zones called the continental shelves. These shelves slope away from land and into the deeper parts of the ocean.

Crisscrossing the ocean floor are many deep spots. The deepest of these that we know of is the Challenger Deep, in the Pacific Ocean. Here, the ocean floor is 35,810 ft (10,915 m) below the water's surface. That is farther below sea level than many jet airliners fly above it!

Normal submarines cannot go this deep – only specially built submersibles can make the journey.

This submersible can operate 3000 ft (910 m) under the water. Here, it is in shallow water, before a deep dive

Deep divers

The earliest submarines were built mostly as warships that could seek and destroy enemy ships without being detected.

▲ *Drebbel's underwater craft may have looked like this. A rowboat was covered with waterproof canvas, and sacks inside were flooded with water to sink the craft just below the waterline.*

The first underwater craft was built by Dutch inventor Cornelius van Drebbel. He crossed the Thames River in London, underwater, in 1620.

▶ *This two-person electric submarine was a French design. It was tested in 1889.*

Battery compartment

The first submarine warship was the *Turtle*. It was built in 1775, during the American Revolution, as the rebels' secret weapon to attack a British ship. The *Turtle* was used to drill a hole in the enemy ship's bottom, and attach an explosive to sink it. Unfortunately for the rebels, the British ship had a metal-plated hull that was too tough for the drill.

▶ *Crew members load supplies aboard British C-class subs before a patrol in 1906.*

◀ *Ezra Lee went in the* Turtle *to attack the HMS Eagle, in 1776. He turned the propeller using a hand wheel.*

Submarine design improved greatly with the *Holland*, launched in 1898 and named after its Irish-American builder. The sub had advanced features, such as fin-like **hydroplanes** that allowed it to dive and climb like an underwater airplane. It used gasoline engines to cruise on the surface and electric motors when underwater.

Holland's submarine

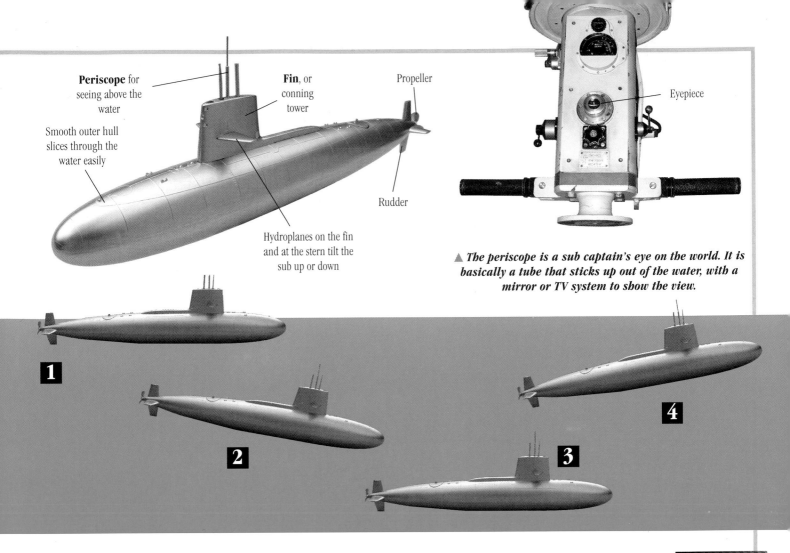

Periscope for seeing above the water

Smooth outer hull slices through the water easily

Fin, or conning tower

Propeller

Rudder

Hydroplanes on the fin and at the stern tilt the sub up or down

Eyepiece

▲ The periscope is a sub captain's eye on the world. It is basically a tube that sticks up out of the water, with a mirror or TV system to show the view.

1

2

3

4

▲ This picture sequence shows:
1 Sub on surface with blown ballast tanks.
2 The tanks are flooded with water to make the sub heavier so it sinks.

3 The sub now cruises at a set level underwater.
4 Water in the ballast tanks is released. The sub gets lighter and rises to the surface.

Submarines must control their **buoyancy** to rise or fall in the water. To dive, a set of ballast tanks are flooded with water, making the submarine move downward. To come to the surface, the same tanks are blown, or emptied of water. Powerful air pumps force the water out of the tanks. With air instead of water in the ballast tanks, the sub is more buoyant and rises.

By changing the amount of air and water in the tanks, the sub can rise or fall in the water quickly or slowly, as needed.

When was the first successful sub attack?

The first successful sub attack was in 1864, during the American Civil War. The Hunley was a metal tube, big enough for eight men and a captain. There was no engine. The crew turned hand cranks, which spun the propeller. The Hunley went into battle armed with a spar torpedo, an explosive attached to the end of a long wooden pole, which stuck out the front of the sub. The attack, against the USS Housatonic, went as planned, except for a deadly error – the torpedo exploded too soon, and both ships were sunk. All the crew on the Hunley died in the attack.

In 1998, a replica of the sub was made for a TV program. Two years later, the original wreck was raised from the water. The wreck is now on display in the Warren Lasch conservation center, in South Carolina.

▼ The Hunley replica being lowered into the water, for its TV appearance.

Subs at war

Submarines were deadly weapons used during both world wars to sink thousands of ships. Submarines and their crews were also at risk.

▲ *Many submarines were armed with a deck gun as well as torpedoes.*

During World War I, from 1914 to 1918, submarines were sent into battle. German subs were called U-boats. The most successful U-boat, the U-35, sunk over 300 ships to the bottom of the sea. Submarines and their crews also faced dangers. For example, a sub might graze against a **mine** floating in the water. A mine was a powerful bomb that exploded if anything touched it.

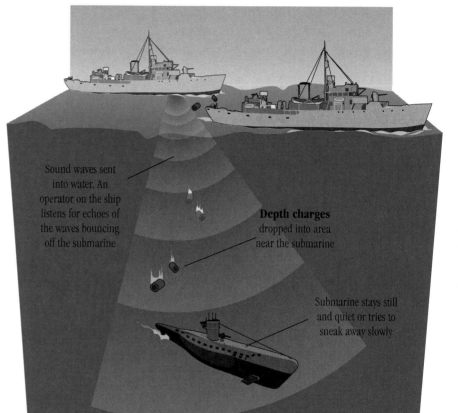

Sound waves sent into water. An operator on the ship listens for echoes of the waves bouncing off the submarine

Depth charges dropped into area near the submarine

Submarine stays still and quiet or tries to sneak away slowly

▶ *A submarine was in danger if ships on the surface could track it by underwater sonar detection equipment. Ships made repeated runs over the sub, dropping depth charges each time to detect its whereabouts.*

▲ *The sinking of a cargo ship in World War II, moments after being hit by a torpedo. This picture was taken through the submarine commander's attack periscope.*

The weapon that turned submarines into war machines was the torpedo, perfected by Robert Whitehead, who sold the idea to the British in 1871. In World War II, from 1939 to 1945, submarines on both sides torpedoed many ships. In just one month in 1942, German U-boats sank 91 ships in the Atlantic Ocean. Allied forces soon put new anti-submarine weapons into service. These included aircraft, which fired rockets at a surfaced sub. Ships were armed with the hedgehog, a weapon that fired 24 bombs at a time towards a sub. Depth charges made large explosions underwater, and often needed only a near miss to sink a sub, or force the crew to surrender.

Torpedo

◀ *A torpedo, ready to go into a launch tube on a Russian Foxtrot sub. The torpedo is blown out of the tube by a blast of air. In the water, the torpedo's own engines take over.*

Sonar stands for sound navigation and ranging. There are two types of sonar, active and passive. Active sonar signals sound similar to a dolphin's high-pitched clicks in the water. Dolphins hear reflected echoes from objects, as the clicking sound waves bounce off them. Active sonar sends out ghostly "ping" sounds. A trained operator listens for the returning echoes.

Passive sonar uses underwater microphones to listen for noises underwater, such as turning propellers or an approaching torpedo.

Dolphins make clicking sounds to get a sound picture of the water landscape around them

▲ *Russian Foxtrot subs were used during the Cold War. The attack periscope (marked by arrow) was very slim to avoid being spotted by the enemy.*

◄ *Foxtrots had folding hydroplanes and a massive sonar system behind the silver-coated areas in the forward section.*

Some submarines were miniature in size, built to sneak into enemy harbors and sink ships at anchor. British Chariots were little more than torpedoes with two seats. But German Beavers were real miniature subs, complete with a tiny fin, or conning tower.

After World War II came the 45-year-long Cold War, in which communist and capitalist countries competed to control the world. Subs of both sides cruised the seas, ready to attack if the Cold War threats turned into real war. Many subs had diesel-electric engines, others used nuclear power.

▶ *The Beaver could carry a torpedo on each side of its hull. Next to the periscope it had a snorkel. This was a breathing tube enabling the diesel engine to take in air when the sub was just below the surface.*

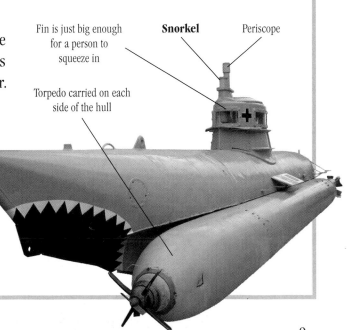

Fin is just big enough for a person to squeeze in

Snorkel   Periscope

Torpedo carried on each side of the hull

Nuclear submarine

A new age in submarine design began when the nuclear sub USS *Nautilus* was launched in 1954. Nuclear power allows a submarine to travel underwater for months at a time, with no need to refuel.

◀ *Modern subs have a sleek hull, shaped for high underwater speeds.*

▲ *The* Nautilus *had a crew of 105 sailors. The sub was 324 ft (99 m) long and could travel underwater at over 22 mph (35 km/h).*

Until the 1950s, submarines mostly used oil-fueled diesel engines. The diesel engines charged batteries, which powered the electric motors the sub used when underwater. The batteries needed recharging often, so World War II subs had to move to the surface and run on diesel power. Above the water they were a target for attacks. Nuclear power changed all this.

▶ *Nuclear submarines are the biggest machines under the sea. When ready for patrol, this newly built sub will be armed with Trident long-range missiles.*

▲ *In 1959, the USS* Skate *surfaced at the North Pole, using its strong metal fin to punch through the ice.*

In a nuclear-powered submarine, a **reactor** heats water in boiler tubes, similar to a high-tech steam engine. The reactor uses hot uranium fuel, which has to be carefully monitored, because it is radioactive. Radioactive materials emit radiation, invisible rays which cause sickness or death if they enter the human body in even very small quantities. Submarine reactors are generally safe and the military benefits are important.

◀ *Divers suit-up for a mission outside a sub. Divers may be sent out to fix problems, such as a loose plate, a jammed hatch or, very rarely, a broken propeller.*

Unlike the diesel engine, a reactor does not need air, so a nuclear sub can stay underwater for months at a time. Steam from the reactor spins turbines, which are much quieter than diesels, making the sub harder to locate. Even the biggest nuclear sub can travel at 35 mph (55 km/h) or more.

▲ *Inside a submarine:*
1 Red lights are used in the control room from dusk to dawn, for night vision through the periscope.
2 Looking through the periscope.
3 Crew members called planesmen control the angle of the sub, when going up or down.
4 The main control panel is packed with instruments.

Missile-armed nuclear submarines often go on patrol for ten weeks or more. After diving, the sub heads out for its cruise area, far out in the ocean. Regular duties on board include navigation and equipment checks plus day-to-day chores, such as cleaning and polishing. The crew goes on alert for missile-firing drill, when everything short of an actual launch is practiced.

Off-duty crew keep fit in a small exercise gym, study for exams, play cards, or watch movies in the small theater. The crew breathe fresh air and drink clean water by using special machines, which extract air and water from sea water.

▼ *The Ohio-class U.S. sub carries up to 24 long-range missiles in vertical tubes.*

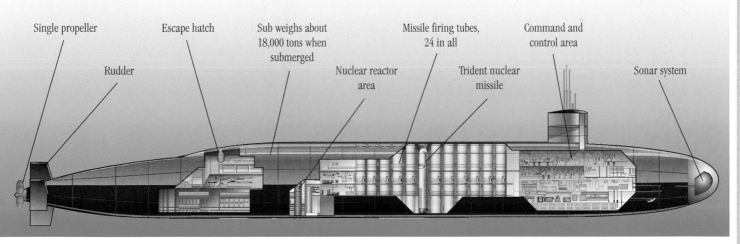

Single propeller

Escape hatch

Sub weighs about 18,000 tons when submerged

Missile firing tubes, 24 in all

Command and control area

Rudder

Nuclear reactor area

Trident nuclear missile

Sonar system

How does nuclear power work in a sub?

Nuclear subs work by simple principles, but they are very expensive and difficult to make.

The nuclear reactor heats water in a system of pipes to make high-pressure steam. The steam spins turbines, which are linked to the sub's propeller shaft by gears. As the turbine blades spin around, the gears turn the propeller.

The turbines also produce electricity for the sub's heat, light, and electronics. Everything depends on a smooth flow of steam from the nuclear reactor.

Nuclear fuel lasts a long time. A reactor needs refueling only every five years or so. The spent, or used, fuel is still dangerous and has to be stored in special facilities.

▼ *Spent nuclear fuel is kept in underground storage areas.*

Subs today

▲ *The British HMS* Vanguard *carries Trident missiles, as well as torpedoes.*

Submarines today are far bigger than the ones used in World War II. They can be armed with missiles as well as torpedoes.

Modern submarines are fast and quiet. They can dive deep to avoid detection. Many subs are still made with diesel engines, with electric motors for submerged travel. Diesels may seem old-fashioned, but they are fairly cheap to build, making them affordable for smaller countries. There are more than 40 navies around the world with submarines in their fleets.

▶ *U.S. Seawolf-class subs are nuclear hunter-killers, designed to seek and destroy enemy subs. Quietness is vital and these subs are as quiet at high speed as some earlier subs were while tied up at port!*

◀ *One use of this sub would be for top-secret missions where it surfaces near a shoreline and delivers a special-forces team. The team uses fast rubber boats to reach land quickly. Such missions are usually carried out at night, so the sub can come and go unseen.*

Today's submarines give their crews a little more living room and comfort than earlier designs. U.S. Seawolf-class subs have a crew of 134 members. Officers sleep three to a stateroom. Other crew members share the 40 bunk areas, with bunks stacked four-high. Only the captain has a single room. Everyone aboard has good food, served from the sub's **galley**.

Russia's Typhoon-class subs are the largest submarines. A Typhoon is 560 ft (170 m) long and weighs around 26,000 tons when submerged. The size has some advantages for the crew, especially when they are off-duty. The sub has a rest area with comfy lounge seats and special lighting which matches the colors of daylight. A giant photo of the Russian countryside is mounted on the wall to remind the sailors of home.

Missiles are carried in tubes in front of the fin

Large fin

Control room is in this area

Twin propellers

▲ *U.S. crewmen listen carefully to their sonar equipment during an exercise.*

▶ *This diesel-electric sub was built in Sweden. Here it floats in an icy Swedish port ready to be delivered to the Singapore navy, in southeast Asia.*

The latest torpedoes are very fast. They can reach speeds of 60 mph (100 km/h) or more. They are also smart, with on-board computers that can track a target. The British Navy's Spearfish torpedo trails a fine wire during the first stages of an attack. Steering signals pass along the wire from the sub to guide the torpedo towards its target. Once the torpedo's built-in sonar detects the enemy, the Spearfish runs on its own, speeding up to attack, twisting and turning, before closing in and exploding.

▼ *Torpedoes are a standard weapon, carried aboard all navy submarines.*

◀ *Long-range missiles are fired while a sub is underwater. This Trident II can carry several nuclear warheads. Just one warhead can destroy an entire city.*

▲ Cruise missiles *are fired out of vertical tubes. A few seconds after launch, small wings pop out and a jet engine starts up.*

Sub hunters

▲ **Sonobuoys** *with sensitive underwater microphones can be dropped by aircraft into the sea.*

Submarines usually cruise slowly and quietly to avoid detection by enemy forces. Sonar systems detect noise and are the main way of locating another submarine.

Underwater operations are like a deadly game of military "cat and mouse." A sub may hunt for ships or subs, but at the same time, it is also being hunted by enemy forces.

▲ *Hunter-killer subs seek enemy subs. The nose section carries a large sonar system.*

Sonar is the main way of finding a submarine. Passive sonar is used more, because underwater listening equipment is silent. The pinging made by active sonar gives a sub's position away instantly to anyone using passive sonar.

Below the top casing is an inner pressure hull. It is built extra-strong, to keep water out

When a sonar operator picks up a noise, skill and experience are needed. The sounds may come from a submarine, or from whales or fish. Shifting currents may also affect sounds, making them move or even disappear. Only a trained operator can tell the sounds apart.

◀ *A submarine can sink surface ships with torpedoes, or with missiles. This* **Harpoon** *missile is shown being test-fired.*

► *The Merlin helicopter carries a big load of sub-hunt equipment, including sonar, sonobuoys, and missiles.*

▲ *Today, submarines operate with other forces as part of a total military operation. Satellites and aircraft relay orders and information between submarines, surface ships, and land forces.*

Hunting a submarine by helicopter is a high-tech job. After liftoff from a carrier ship, a helicopter crew drops sonobuoys into the sea. A radio in the buoy transmits underwater sounds to the helicopter. A dunking sonar is lowered by cable into the water, while the helicopter hovers overhead. If a sub is tracked, the helicopter can then attack with a lightweight torpedo.

Long-range patrol planes are also used as sub-hunters. As well as sonobuoys, they may use **MAD** (Magnetic Anomaly Detector) equipment. This detects change in magnetism underwater, caused by the metal in a submarine's hull.

What are the fastest submarines?

The world's navies keep the exact performance of their latest subs a top secret. Most experts agree that Russia's Akula, or Shark, subs are probably the fastest, with a top speed of nearly 40 mph (65 km/h).

The Akula is packed with high-tech equipment, such as a sound-absorbing coating on the hull, which makes the sub very quiet. The Akula also has sonar jamming equipment, and can launch a small torpedo that makes sub sounds. This acts as a decoy, allowing the Akula to slip away unseen.

Rear fin holds sonar equipment and a rudder

Rescue mission

▲ *A* **diving bell** *can be used to lower rescue divers to a damaged sub.*

U nderwater patrols are generally routine operations for submarines and their crews. Occasionally something may go wrong and then a sub can get into trouble very quickly.

There are many dangers when a submarine is underwater. A leak in the hull, a damaged rudder, or engine failure can all cause trouble. Many subs can dive to 2000 ft (610 m) safely, but if they go much deeper, the pressure hull may start to leak, flooding the sub with water.

▲ *A* **DSRV** *can be carried in a cargo jet. Once underwater the DSRV locks on to a damaged sub using a watertight lock.*

In shallow water, crew can use an escape hatch and swim to the surface. In deeper water, they have to send a distress signal, then wait for rescue.

▲ *Rubber escape suits were used on Russian Foxtrot subs built in the 1960s. Wearing them, crew members could escape through the hatch into the water.*

T he deep submergence rescue vehicle, or **DSRV**, can reach a trapped sub in deep water. The DSRV can go down to about 3500 ft (1000 m), lock on to an escape hatch and carry sailors to safety, 24 at a time. Many subs have crews of 100 or more, so a rescue could take many hours.

Another type of rescue machine is now being designed. This smaller craft would be lowered on a cable from a rescue ship to the damaged sub. It could be assembled and ready for action in eighteen hours.

Russia's *Kursk* was a giant submarine that met disaster in August 2000. During military exercises, several explosions, probably from misfiring torpedoes, blasted a massive hole in the sub's front section. Moments later, the submarine was sinking to the bottom of the sea.

Rescuers tried to enter the *Kursk* to save the crew, but the sub's hatch was damaged. After ten days, Norwegian divers managed to open the hatch, but found the sub flooded. The entire crew of 118 sailors were dead.

???

What about medical problems?

Nuclear submarines often stay on patrol for three months. With crews that range from 80 to 130 or more, there are plenty of minor illnesses that need treatment by the sub's doctor. For really serious cases, the captain may decide to call for help. The sub will cruise to a mid-ocean meeting spot, and a medical team may be flown in to assist, or the sick crew member can be taken off the submarine for treatment in hospital.

▶ *A doctor is winched, or lowered down, to treat a sick crew member. The helicopter can take the patient off the sub, if needed.*

▼ *This diagram of the* Kursk *shows:*
1 *Huge hole blown in the forward section by exploding torpedoes.*
2 *Torpedo storage area. Up to 24 torpedoes are normally carried.*
3 *Command area shown flooded. Water soon filled the rest of the sub as the rear sank to the sea floor.*
4 *Nuclear power plants would have been shut down after the explosion.*
5 *Steam turbines supply electricity*

for the two propellers. When the turbines stopped, light and heat would have come from batteries.
6 *Escape hatch. Some sailors tried to use it, but could not get through the flooded escape tube.*
7 *Each side of the sub stores cruise missiles in two rows of twelve.*
8 *The submarine is about 505 ft (154 m) long. This diagram shows it compared to a Boeing 747 airliner.*

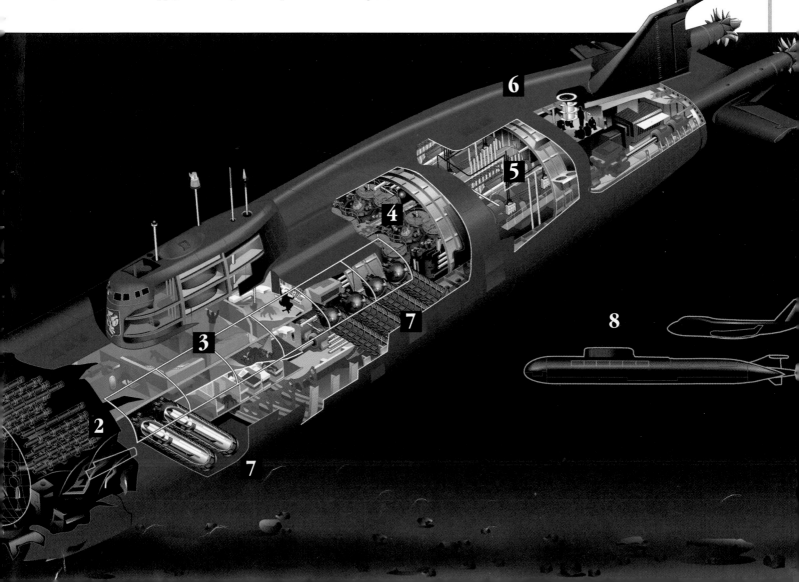

Voyage to the deep

Exploring the ocean floors is a job for specially made research craft. These are machines built to survive the crushing pressure of water at extreme depths.

▲ *In 1930, ocean explorer William Beebe made the first submersible trip in a metal* bathysphere *that was lowered into the water by a cable.*

NEW YORK ZOOLOGICAL SOCIETY BATHYSPHERE

Main section filled with gasoline, which weighs less than water

Rear fin to keep craft steady

▲ *The* Trieste *worked like an underwater airship. Instead of a gas bag, it used gasoline, which is lighter than water.*

Piccard and Walsh stayed in the crew sphere during the dive

The deepest dive ever was in a strange-looking craft called the *Trieste*. In 1960, Jacques Piccard and Donald Walsh started on a trip to the Challenger Deep, in the Mariana Trench, the deepest part of the Pacific Ocean. The underwater explorers were descending to a dangerous depth where the water pressure measures more than 14,000 lb/sq inch (1000 kg/sq cm), enough to crush an ordinary submarine. Almost five hours after leaving the surface, lights on the *Trieste* showed the bottom coming into view. One of the first things Piccard and Walsh saw was a strange-looking fish. Until then, no one knew if ocean life existed at this depth.

◄ *The fangtooth fish is one of the many strange-looking marine animals that live in the dark depths of the oceans. This species has been found as deep as 16,400 ft (5000 m).*

Hatchet fish are another deep-water species. Their bodies are almost transparent

What other tools do researchers use?

Many devices are used for deep-sea exploring, including a 43-inch (110-cm) long probe called Palace. Hundreds of these are dropped into the oceans. Each one sinks to a depth of 6560 ft (2000 m), where it drifts for ten days.

Probes record such things as water saltiness, temperature, and current speed. The probes bob to the surface to send information to a satellite, which then relays the data to a research team on land.

Deep-ocean research has revealed some amazing discoveries. **Black smokers**, which are caused by super-hot molten rock leaking through vents in the ocean floor, are just one discovery. Deep-ocean life, such as gigantic crabs, cluster around the vents. Scientists first explored vents in 1979, and are still finding new species gathered around them.

Some researchers are using robotic subs to look for marine life. They want to find out if there are microscopic life forms living in the fractured rocks *below* the ocean floor!

◄ *Hot fluid bubbles out of the ocean floor at 760°F (390°C). The warmth and minerals from a black smoker attracts worms, crabs, and other ocean animals.*

▲ *Diver-explorers walking on the sea floor, as imagined by the artist who illustrated the book 20,000 Leagues under the Sea, in the 1880s.*

► *The Alvin can go to a depth of 13,000 ft (3960 m). There is room inside for three people. They sit in a cramped steel sphere under the fin. This craft has gone on many underwater explorations.*

Finding wrecks

Searching for sunken ships and bringing up the treasures they hold is fascinating for divers and researchers. Today's equipment makes searching easy.

The *Titanic* ocean liner sank in the North Atlantic in 1912. Its final resting spot remained a mystery until 1985, when the *Titanic* was found by a team in the submersible *Alvin*. A smaller unmanned craft, *Jason Jr*, explored inaccessible areas of the wreck, under control from the *Alvin*. They found many surprises. Most of the *Titanic*'s wood fittings had been eaten away, but a champagne cork was left untouched!

▲ *The robotic vehicle* Jason Jr *explores a hatchway on the* Titanic, *deep in the Atlantic Ocean.*

▼ *There are many wrecks around the world. This one lies in shallow water in the Caribbean Sea.*

▲ *The* Royal Oak *lies 90 ft (30 m) deep. This British battleship was one of the largest ships sunk during World War II. The ship's guns are covered with sea growths.*

Other wrecks include those of sunken warships, which may be either old sailing boats or more recent remains from twentieth-century sea battles. In 1939, the *Royal Oak* battleship was torpedoed by a U-boat in chilly waters off Scotland. The ship was made a war grave, in honor of the 833 men who died when it sank. The rusty wreck is still leaking oil and there are plans to go down and drain the tanks before local wildlife suffers.

◄ *British inventor Charles Babbage designed this submersible in 1855, to clear sunken warships from a harbor. It was a large upside-down metal bowl that held air for divers.*

▲ Remote-operated vehicles (ROVs) are controlled from the surface. Underwater TV cameras show the undersea view to an operator. Signals are sent to and from the ROV through a cable. Treasures found on old shipwrecks include valuable gold coins. The coins shown above are over 400 years old.

Bringing up a cargo of old gold coins or parts of a sunken wreck is called salvage. Private collectors and museums are often eager to add these rare items to their displays. There are often surprises for recovery teams. The wreck of a Danish ship, sunk in 1786, concealed a cargo of reindeer hides perfectly preserved under a layer of thick mud! Divers used to care little about retrieving anything except money. Sometimes they used explosives or axes to tear wrecks apart to get at the valuables. Today's researchers are more careful to preserve these historical treasures.

Large eels often hide in old wrecks

How does breathing gear work?

Many shallow-water wrecks are best explored by skin divers, who use the breathing gear that was first developed in 1943 by the French underwater explorer Jacques Cousteau. Cousteau named it the aqualung. Today it is known as scuba, which stands for self-contained underwater breathing apparatus. A metal tank sends air through a rubber pipe to a mouthpiece. This has an "on-demand" valve that feeds air to the diver when it is needed. Scuba is easy to use. Divers just suck in through their mouths, and the correct amount of air flows.

Underwater workers

W hen divers need to work for a long time or at great depths, hard suits are used. These are designed so that a diver can work in cold water.

Important equipment used by different industries is placed under the sea. Oil and gas companies install drilling machinery and build pipelines in the oceans. Communications companies lay telephone cables between continents. Military planners use seabed listening stations to check on the movements of submarines.

Equipment maintenance and repairs require humans to work underwater.

▲ *The first diving suit was made in 1797 in Germany. A metal dome covered the head. Tight straps kept the suit waterproof.*

▶ *The newt suit is like underwater astronaut's gear. A large backpack carries two electric thruster motors which turn the suit's two propellers.*

H ard suits have some advantages over scuba gear. A very important one is that a diver can work in comfort, even in cold winter seas. The newt suit is built for working 1000 ft (305 m) for eight hours at a time. It is a heavy machine, weighing 833 lb (378 kg) when it is out of the water. Once submerged, the suit becomes weightless. On the seabed, a diver can move like an underwater astronaut, using the two battery-powered propeller thrusters mounted on the backpack.

Thrusters mounted on each side of the backpack

◀ *This 1960s science-fiction magazine showed underwater soldiers wearing bulky suits that look much like today's newt suit.*

▶ *Globe Probe is a two-person diving bell, used for undersea maintenance. This device can safely go 1500 ft (460 m) deep.*

How do you operate an ROV?

Remote-operated vehicles operate in a similar way to a slow-motion video game. The operator normally sits in front of TV screens on a surface ship. One screen shows ROV data, such as its power levels and position. Other screens show different views from cameras mounted on the ROV.

The operator controls an ROV's movements using a joystick, with a keypad to change camera angles.

The job is harder than it sounds. The TV picture is often dark and fuzzy, making it difficult to check how far away things are. There is also no sense of touch when handling objects with the robot arm and grippers.

◄ *Powerful lights give TV cameras a bright picture when this ROV goes underwater to work. It can pick up samples with the robot arm under the hull.*

Manipulator arm under hull

◄ *This robotic sub tracks the sea floor automatically. Information is sent to a surface ship by floating radio transmitters.*

► *A massive metal gantry, or crane, lifts a robotic sub from a surface ship into the water.*

Remote-operated vehicles (ROVs) now work on many jobs that used to be done by divers, and are much safer for deep-sea work. An ROV is usually controlled through a two-way electronic cable from a surface ship, or sometimes from a submersible, such as the *Alvin*. TV cameras are the operator's eyes, and robotic manipulators are the arms and hands.

Oceans in peril?

Researchers use subs to keep track of what is happening in the world's oceans. Dangers to the seas include pollution and overfishing.

▲ Oil or chemical spills can be deadly for sea life. Here, poisoned fish lie washed up on a seashore.

▼ This ROV is used for checking pipelines and other underwater systems in the North Sea.

Exploration for new oil fields is now taking place underwater. This is a danger to the environment, because a big oil leak could be very difficult to control. Some companies use ROVs to monitor their work underwater. These TV-equipped submersibles are used to check that the surrounding seabed is not affected by the drilling.

Oil and chemical spills, sometimes caused by shipwrecks, are a danger to sea life. Some ships leak for years. ROVs, like the one shown at right, can check leaks, and oil and gas pipelines, to make sure that they are safe.

This oil rig stands on the sea floor. The oil-bearing rock may be thousands of feet below this

Nuclear submarines are very reliable, but if there is a serious problem with the reactor, deadly uranium fuel may leak into the sea. In 2000, the British Royal Navy had to recall its entire force of twelve nuclear hunter-killer subs. The problem was that the reactor cooling pipes in one of the subs had cracked. All the subs were checked because cracks would lead to overheating in the nuclear power plants, and what the experts call "a catastrophic failure" of the system.

◄ There are hundreds of rigs taking oil from under continental shelves. Even so, the main risk of spills is from ships carrying oil. Oil tankers sometimes hit rocks, collide with other ships, or run aground.

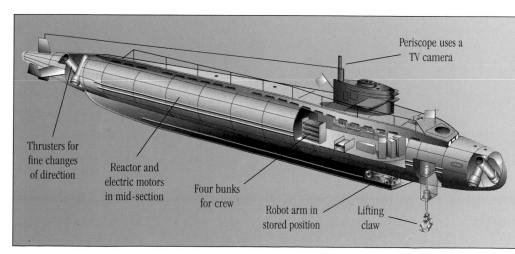

▼ Powerful lights are needed in deep water. Sunlight penetrates only the upper layers of the ocean, where most sea animals live.

Understanding how the oceans work, and how they are affected by humans is a constant job for researchers. Information may come from diver's samples, or from satellites, such as Seasat. This satellite can monitor pollution and seawater temperatures from high above our planet.

Another research machine is the Autosub. This is a robotic submarine that looks like a small torpedo. An Autosub is packed with instruments that enable it to glide under the ice around Antarctica. Researchers want to find out what sort of sea life can live in these unexplored regions.

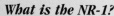

Periscope uses a TV camera

Thrusters for fine changes of direction

Reactor and electric motors in mid-section

Four bunks for crew

Robot arm in stored position

Lifting claw

What is the NR-1?

The NR-1 is the world's only nuclear-powered research sub. This U.S. Navy craft has several jobs, including searching for sunken ships.

NR-1 has a robotic arm which is used to grasp underwater objects. A metal claw extends down for lifting things off the seabed.

The sub can operate at a depth of 2375 ft (724 m), which allows it to carry out research on the continental shelves, although not on the far deeper ocean bottom.

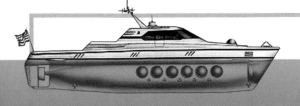

What's next?

▲ *The Seattle 1000 luxury sub has underwater portholes running along the sides and a big transparent section to see the view ahead.*

Subs for the oil, gas, and tourist industries need to be cheap to buy and operate. Navies need more powerful submarines that dive deeper and are quieter.

Submarines are expensive to build and use. There are enough people wanting to visit the deep sea world that tourist subs could be profitable. The Seattle 1000 luxury sub is a tourist submarine. It can dive to 1000 ft (305 m) and can carry ten people. The builders have plans for a bigger sub called the Phoenix. This will be 213 ft (65 m) long and cost $75 million to make. Diesel engines will be used on the surface, with electric motors for diving.

◀ *This ROV is the size of a football. It has revolving fins, instead of a propeller, that move it forward.*

▶ *This robotic fish has a twisting body and tail, designed to move through the water just like the real thing.*

▲ *The Deep Flight two-seater from Hawkes Ocean Technologies is like an underwater fighter plane.*

Fish are very efficient swimmers, so some researchers are studying how they swim. The researchers hope to learn how to make machines that move faster and more efficiently through water. For instance, a robotic fish flexes its body to produce swimming strokes like a real fish, instead of using a propeller. The skin is made of stainless-steel mesh and lycra fabric, with battery-powered motors in the nose. The fins are used for steering, and controlled by a human operator outside the tank.

What about a supersonic sub?

A supersonic sub sounds unlikely but may be possible one day. It would use a rocket instead of propellers and produce a bubble of water vapor instead of liquid around the sub. The sub would not have to push water aside and could go very fast. Experiments have shown that a flat nose can push water aside at an angle that allows a vapor bubble to form. The Russians made a torpedo using this idea in the early 1990s, called the Shkval. It can reach over 230 mph (370 km/h). In 1997, a U.S. team fired a small projectile through the water at over 3460 mph (5570 km/h)!

The front of this supersonic sub is flat, not rounded

S ilence and high speeds are the main goals for navy submarine builders. A future non-nuclear sub could have smooth and quiet turbine engines, fueled by natural gas. The turbines could be used underwater, without needing electric motors. A special hull made of many fine tubes would be used to store the natural gas.

Thrusters give forward power

Hydroplanes control climbs, dives, and turns

◀ *This two-seat deep-sea machine is a design for the near future. The machine can zoom, roll, and turn under the sea, just like an aircraft can perform aerobatics in the air.*

Crew lie on their chests inside the see-through domes

▶ *A future sub moves silently through enemy waters. Ultra-quiet turbine engines burn gas that is stored in the outer hull. Exhaust gases are stored in tubes, so there are no bubbles to give away the sub's position.*

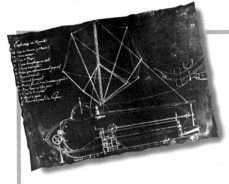

Time track

A list of some important dates in deep-sea machines and research, from the work of early pioneers to nuclear submarines, and into the future.

▲ *Loading a torpedo aboard an Akula submarine.*

▲ *Robert Fulton built the Nautilus sub in 1801, with money from the French emperor Napoleon. The sub had a sail on the surface and a propeller turned by hand underwater.*

About 323 B.C. The earliest recorded underwater craft was used by Alexander the Great. It is thought to have been a large barrel with glass port holes.

1620s Dutch inventor Cornelius van Drebbel builds an underwater craft which travels under the Thames River in London. The oars passed through a watertight, leather dome. How the oarsmen breathed properly remains Drebbel's secret. He may have found a chemical that gave off oxygen. The gas could have been kept in a bottle and released when anyone needed air.

1715 John Lethbridge makes a wood and iron diving suit, which can be lowered 66 ft (20 m) into water by a cable.

▲ *A design to show how Jules Verne's fictional Nautilus might have looked. Verne equipped his fictional submarine with electric motors, and even an organ for Captain Nemo to play in his spare time!*

1776 During the American Revolution, the first sub attack is made. The *Turtle* tries to sink a British ship with a gunpowder bomb. The attack fails, but the sub returns to base safely.

1819 First diving suit is perfected by a German, Augustus Siebe. One problem was that water could leak in if the diver bent over. In 1837, Siebe produced a fully closed suit. Suits with a similar design remain in service today.

1863 First powered submarine, the French-built *Plongeur,* is driven by compressed air and is fitted with a set of hydroplanes to control its angle in the water. It can dive to about 20 ft (6 m) but is not stable.

1864 The Confederate Army's *Hunley* is the first submarine to sink an enemy ship, the USS *Housatonic.* The *Hunley* also sinks in the attack, killing all eight men on board the craft.

1866 Robert Whitehead invents the first motorized torpedo. The torpedo will go on to become the standard attack weapon used by all military submarines.

1870 French writer Jules Verne publishes his novel *20,000 Leagues Under the Sea*. This is a science-fiction adventure which features an advanced submarine called the *Nautilus.* Verne names his fictional sub after Fulton's model of 1801.

1872 First expedition to research the deep sea, by HMS *Challenger*. During a long voyage scientists map sea floors and collect marine specimens.

1879 An English clergyman builds a submarine called The *Resurgam,* that is powered by a steam engine.

1886 The French *Gymnote* is the first submarine to be really successful. It is driven by electric motors and has a cigar-shaped hull. It also has hydroplanes which work well. Tests continue for several years.

1897 The USS *Holland* is launched. It is powered by gasoline engines on the surface, and has electric motors for running submerged.

1898 The U.S. Navy buys five 120-ton submarines designed by John P. Holland, the Irish-American designer of the USS *Holland*.

1899 The French *Narwal* sub adds a double hull for safety.

1900 The first Holland-design sub is delivered to the U.S. Navy. A year later, the British Royal Navy also orders its first Holland sub.

1904 A Japanese torpedo attack on a Russian surface fleet establishes the torpedo as the sub's ideal weapon.

1904 French sub *Aigette* is the first to have a diesel engine.

1914-1918 In World War I, diesel subs are widely introduced. German subs, called U-boats, attack supply ships crossing the Atlantic Ocean.

1930 William Beebe and Otis Barton make a dive in their bathysphere to 1400 ft (459 m). Four years later they go to 3028 ft (993 m). In 1948, Barton dives to reach a depth of 4050 ft (1328 m).

1930s Miniature subs are developed in Italy and Japan. Other small craft in World War II were used by Britain and Germany.

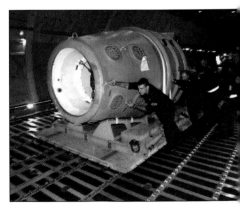

▲ *The DSRV rescue craft can be carried in a cargo jet. This enables it to be taken to the site of a sunken ship or sub quickly.*

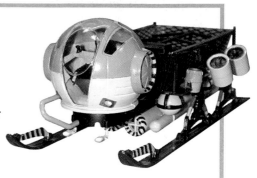

▲ *The TV series "seaQuest" featured a manned deep-ocean vehicle. Designs like this may be built in the future. Robotic craft will be used even more for dangerous deep-water work.*

▲ *Scuba diving gear was first used by the French underwater pioneers Jacques Cousteau and Emil Gagnon in 1943. For the first time, people could go underwater for long stays, without wearing bulky suits.*

1933   The snorkel, a breathing tube for engines, is developed by Jan Wichers, from Holland. It does not go into general use immediately. The first military sub to use one is the German U-264 in 1943.

1939-1945 Submarines go to battle on all sides during World War II. Duty on a sub becomes very dangerous after anti-sub weapons are developed. By the end of the war, the Germans had built 1162 U-boats, which sank a total of 2828 Allied ships. Most of these U-boats are also sunk during the war, with many human deaths.

1944   First use of MAD (Magnetic Anomaly Detector) for submarine hunting. MAD equipment can detect the magnetic pattern caused by a sub's metal hull in water. In the same year, the first sonobuoys are developed. They can listen to underwater sounds, detecting the noise of a submarine, such as its engines or turning propellers.

1952   USS *Albacore* is the first submarine to have a smooth, teardrop-shaped hull, designed for high speed when submerged.

1954   The first nuclear-powered submarine, the USS *Nautilus* is launched at a boatyard in Connecticut.

1958   USS *Nautilus* travels under the North Polar ice cap.

1960   Jacques Piccard and Donals Walsh reach the deepest spot underwater in the *Trieste* bathyscaphe. The Challenger Deep, near the Mariana Islands, is 35,800 ft (11,737 m) below the surface. The trip takes nearly five hours, with not much to look at on the way. As Walsh said, "Past 500 ft (164 m) it's pitch-dark." But they spot a flat fish on the bottom just before they land, which proves that life does survive down there.

1962   Experiments in underwater living begin with a project called Conshelf, short for Continental Shelf Station. Two aquanauts spend over a week working in the Conshelf, on the floor of the Mediterranean Sea, near Marseilles in France.

1968   Four researchers spend 60 days in an underwater station during Operation Tektite.

1980   The first U.S. Ohio-class missile submarine is launched. It can carry up to 24 long-range missiles, plus a load of torpedoes.

1980   The first Russian Typhoon-class sub goes into service. This is the world's largest sub, weighing 26,000 tons when submerged.

1990s   Russia puts a super-speed torpedo into service. The Shkval (Squall) can travel at about 230 mph (370 km/h), four times faster than any other torpedo.

1995   The Russian Oscar-class submarine *Kursk* is launched. Oscars are very large military machines – they are about 505 ft (154 m) long, and 60 ft (18.3 m) wide.

2000   *Kursk* sinks in an accident during military exercises. Large explosions, perhaps from a torpedo exploding in the ship, blow a hole in the hull. Despite the efforts from international rescue teams, all the crew are lost.

2001   The *Alvin* and other submersibles continue with underwater research work. There are only four other subs that can take humans down to below 10,000 ft (3279 m). The Russian *Mir I* and *Mir II*, along with the French *Nautile*, can go down to 20,000 ft (6557 m). The Japanese *Shinkai* can reach 21,320 ft (6990 m).

Into the future
2000s   The tourist sub industry slowly increases in size. Several luxury subs are built for private clients.

2000s   Unmanned machines become even more important as companies drill for oil, gas, and minerals in very deep ocean waters. Advanced computer technology enables many to be completely automatic in operation.

2010s   Super-speed torpedoes go into general service in several navies.

2020s   Super-speed technology is developed for crewed craft, leading to a new generation of attack craft.

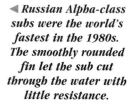

◄ *Russian Alpha-class subs were the world's fastest in the 1980s. The smoothly rounded fin let the sub cut through the water with little resistance.*

▲ *Subs sometimes surface at high speeds, like a whale breaching the surface.*

Glossary

An explanation of the technical terms and concepts used in this book.

▲ *A sub may be taken to a special dry dock for maintenance.*

▲ *A sailor gets ready to seal the hatch of a tourist sub before a dive.*

▼ *A hunter-killer sub and an ASW helicopter meet in mid-ocean.*

ASW
Anti-Submarine Warfare. Present-day equipment includes ships, helicopters, and aircraft, all of which can be equipped with sensitive detectors – and can attack with torpedoes, mines, bombs, or missiles.

Ballast tank
Water tank on a sub that can be filled with or emptied of water or air so that the sub can dive or surface.

Bathysphere
A type of diving machine shaped like a sphere. It is winched down into the sea by a strong cable from a surface ship. The name comes from the Greek word *bathys* meaning deep. The deep-diving *Trieste* was a bathyscaphe, which added another Greek word, *scaphe,* meaning boat.

Black smoker
Describes an ocean-floor vent, where hot molten rock boils into the water. A mixture of various chemicals in the hot fluid turns it into a dark smoke colour. This heat (the ocean floor zone is normally only about 2.5°C) attracts a wide range of bottom-dwelling animals.

Buoyancy
How an object floats in the water. A high-buoyancy object will float, a low-buoyancy object will sink.

Class
A number of submarines, or surface ships, that are built to the same design. For example, the *Kursk* was an Oscar-class submarine.

Continental shelf
The fairly shallow waters that surround the continents. They are not much deeper than 656 ft (200 m) but may extend a long way from the coastline. The edge of a shelf slopes to the ocean floor, which is much deeper, at an average of about 12,000 ft (3700 m).

Cruise missile
Type of missile that flies at a low height to make detection and shooting it down difficult. The Tomahawk cruise missiles have a container which splits apart after it is fired. Small wings open out and a jet engine starts up. The Tomahawk then flies to a target according to built-in map instructions.

Depth charge
A bomb that is dropped into the sea to attack a submarine. It explodes under the water, to crack the sub's hull and sink it, or force it to the surface to surrender.

Diving bell
A type of diving equipment that is simply an enclosed vessel, with air pumped through a pipe from the surface. Divers sometimes use a diving bell as a seabed headquarters, returning from time to time for rest and air.

DSRV
Deep Submergence Rescue Vehicle. The DSRV is a U.S. design, but there are others, such as Britain's LR-5 submersible, which can carry up to sixteen sailors at a time.

Fin
The part of a submarine that rises above the main hull. Also known as a conning tower or sail.

Galley
A sub's, or any ship's, kitchen.

Gasoline engine
Type of engine that works like a car engine, using similar fuel. In a submarine, this is a safety risk as fumes from gasoline can catch fire easily. Diesel engines use a heavier oil which is less likely to catch fire. Diesels are also more economical, giving a sub more time between refuelings.

Harpoon
Type of anti-ship or submarine missile.

Hatch
Opening or door in a sub's hull.

Hull
The main body of a submarine or ship.

Hunter-killer
A type of submarine built mainly to hunt other submarines.

Hydroplane

Hydroplane
Small wing-like surfaces on a sub. By changing their angle a sub can dive and climb in the water.

MAD
Magnetic Anomaly Detector. A sensitive instrument that can detect an underwater metal object by its magnetic pattern under the sea.

Manipulator
Mechanical arm used by research submersibles. Usually has a gripper hand that can grasp underwater objects.

Mine
Bomb that floats on or just below the surface. A submarine may set one off by touching it or, with other types of mines, just by coming close to it.

▲ *Even on a big sub, there is not much room on the fin.*

Periscope
A tall pipe that extends up from the fin. Inside is a mirror system, and often a TV camera, so that the captain of a sub can see what is happening above the water's surface. Military subs normally have two periscopes. The attack scope is very slim, to avoid detection. The search scope is bigger and has TV, low-light, and camera systems built in.

Planesmen
The crew in a sub who control the hydroplanes. One sailor works the front planes, another operates the rear planes. Steering is by rudder, which is operated by another crew member.

Reactor
The heart of a sub's nuclear power system. It uses fuel, typically uranium, that heats water to make steam. The steam spins turbine blades, much as wind turns the sails of a windmill. The turbines then turn the sub's propeller through a gearbox. The system also produces electricity for the ship's heating, lighting, and electronics.

ROV
Remote-Operated Vehicle, usually controlled from a surface ship. It may also be called a UUV, or Uncrewed Underwater Vehicle. Robotic machines are being developed that do not need an operator to control their every movement. These are known as AUVs, or Autonomous Underwater Vehicles.

Scuba
Self-contained underwater breathing apparatus. Consists of an air tank and pipe, with a special mouthpiece that feeds air to a diver at exactly the correct pressure. It is also known as an aqualung.

Snorkel
Breathing tube for diesel engines, which need air as well as fuel to work. The snorkel sticks up from the conning tower, next to the periscope. A diesel submarine can cruise just below the surface, much safer than surfacing completely when in battle.

Sonar
System used for detecting objects under water. Active sonar sends out sound pulses, with receivers that can listen for the returning echoes. Passive sonar is silent, and is a listening-only system.

Sonobuoy
An underwater microphone that is used to detect submarines. Helicopters may use dunking sonar, which are lowered from a helicopter on a long cable and dunked below the water's surface.

Spar torpedo
Early type of explosive that was mounted on the end of a long pole, or spar. The *Hunley* carried one of these when it made the first submarine attack in 1864.

Submersible
Describes a slow underwater craft, used mostly for science or industrial jobs. Few of these have a submarine-type smooth casing. High speed is not an important part of a submersible's design, unlike that of a military sub.

Torpedo
Underwater self-propelled weapon. Modern torpedoes can go very fast, usually about 60 mph (100 km/h), and are guided to a target until built-in sonar takes over. Russian Shkval torpedoes use a special system to travel much faster than standard torpedo designs. The Shkval can travel at over 200 mph (322 km/h) but it is not as agile as the slower torpedoes in wide use.

▲ *Front hydroplanes are fitted to each side of the fin on this nuclear submarine. Other subs may have them attached lower down, on the hull.*

▲ *Scuba gear has made diving much easier, and has also helped to make diving a popular sport.*

► *A floating dry dock can be used to lift a sub out of the water for repair work.*

Index

A
American Civil War 7
American Revolution 6, 28
Antarctica 5, 25
anti-submarine weapons 8, 29
aqualung see scuba
ASW (Anti-Submarine Warfare) 30
Atlantic Ocean 4, 5, 8, 20, 28

B
Babbage, Charles 20
ballast tanks 7, 30
Barton, Otis 28
bathyscaphe 29, 30
    Trieste 30
bathysphere 18, 28, 30
Beebe, William 18, 28
black smokers 19, 30

C
Challenger Deep 5, 18, 29
Cold War 9
conning tower see fin
Conshelf (Continental shelf station)
    29
continental shelves 4, 5, 24, 25, 30
Cousteau, Jacques 21, 29

D
depth charge 8, 30
diesel and diesel-electric engines 9,
    10, 12, 13, 26, 28, 30, 31
divers, diving 10, 16, 17, 19, 20, 21,
    22, 30, 31
diving bell 16, 30
    Globe Probe 22
diving suits 22, 28
    newt suit 22
Drebbel, Cornelius van 6, 28
DSRV (Deep Submergence Rescue
    Vehicle) 16, 28, 30

F
fin 7, 9, 10, 13, 15, 18, 19, 29,
    30, 31
Fulton, Robert 28

G
Gagnon, Emil 29
gas 22, 27, 29

H
hatch 10, 11, 16, 17, 30
helicopters 15, 17, 30
HMS *Eagle* 6
HMS *Royal Oak* 20

HMS *Vanguard* 12
Holland, John P. 6, 28
hull 4, 7, 9, 10, 14, 15, 16, 25, 28,
    29, 30, 31
hydroplanes 6, 7, 9, 28, 31

L
Lethbridge, John 28

M
MAD (Magnetic Anomaly Detector)
    15, 29, 31
Mariana Trench 18
Mediterranean Sea 5, 29
mines 8, 30, 31
missiles
    cruise 13, 17, 30
    Harpoon 14
    long-range 13, 29
    Tomahawk cruise 30
    Trident 10, 11, 12, 13

N
North Pole 4, 10, 29
nuclear power 9, 10, 11, 31
nuclear warhead 13

O
oil 22, 24, 29

P
Pacific Ocean 4, 5, 18
periscope 7, 9, 11, 25, 31
Piccard, Jacques 18, 29
pipelines 4, 22, 24
planesmen 11, 31
pollution 24, 25
propellers 7, 10, 11, 13, 28, 29, 31

R
rescue 16-17, 29
research, researchers 2, 4, 5, 19,
    20, 21, 24, 25, 26, 28, 29
robotic fish 26
ROV (Remote-Operated Vehicle) 2,
    21, 23, 24, 26, 31
rudder 7, 11, 15, 16

S
salvage 21
satellites 25
scuba 21, 22, 29, 31
Siebe, Augustus 28
snorkel 9, 29, 31
sonar 8, 9, 11, 13, 14, 15, 31
sonobuoys 14, 15, 29, 31

submersibles 4, 5, 18, 23, 29, 31
    Alvin 5, 19, 20, 23, 29
    Jason Jr 20
    LR-5 30
submarines
    Aigette (French) 28
    Akula (Shark, Russian) 1 28
    Alpha-class (Russian) 29
    Autosub 25
    Beaver (German) 9
    C-class (British) 6
    Chariot (British) 9
    Deep Flight two-seater 26
    Foxtrot (Russian) 8, 9, 16
    Gymnote (French) 28
    HMS *Challenger* 28
    Hunley 7, 28, 31
    hunter-killer 12, 14, 24, 30
    Kursk (Russian) 17, 29, 30
    military 4, 5, 31
    Mir I and *Mir II* (Russian) 29
    Narwal (French) 28
    Nautile (French) 29
    Nautilus 28
    NR-1 25
    nuclear 10-11, 24, 29, 31
    Ohio-class (U.S.) 11, 29
    Oscar-class (Russian) 29, 30
    Plongeur (French) 28
    research 5, 25
    Resurgam 28
    robotic 2, 19, 23, 25
    Seattle 1000 26
    Seawolf-class (U.S.) 12
    Shinkai (Japanese) 29
    tourist 2, 26, 29, 30
    Trieste 18, 29
    Turtle 6, 28
    Typhoon-class (Russian) 13, 29
    U-35 (German) 8
    U-264 (German) 28
    U-boats (German) 8, 20, 28, 29
    USS *Albacore* 29
    USS *Holland* 6, 28
    USS *Nautilus* 10, 29
    USS *Skate* 10

T
Titanic 5, 20
torpedoes 4, 8, 9, 13, 14, 15, 17,
    27, 28, 29, 30, 31
    Shkval (Squall) 29, 31
    spar 7, 31
    Spearfish 13

U
USS *Housatonic* 7, 28

V
vents 19, 30
Verne, Jules 28

W
Walsh, Donald 18, 29
warships 6, 20
Whitehead, Robert 8, 28
Wichers, Jan 29
World War I 8, 28
World War II 8, 10, 20, 28, 29
wrecks 20-21, 24

Acknowledgements
We wish to thank all those individuals and
organizations that have helped create this
publication.

Photographs and diagrams were supplied by:
Alpha Archive
Aqua Technology
Associated Press
Jim Brennan
Terry Cosgrove
Dept of the Navy Sea Systems Command
Electric Boat Corp
Fowler Media Graphics
John E. Gay
Hawkes Ocean Technologies
Hunting Engineering Ltd
David Jefferis
Mark Lawson / The Sunday Times London
Lockheed Martin Corp
Amos Nachoum/CORBIS
Oxford Scientific Films:
    Mark Deeble and Victoria Stone
    Paulo de Oliveira
    Norbert Wu
Gavin Page
Powerdive International
Raytheon Corp
Royal Navy
Science Photo Library:
    Dr. Jeremy Burgess
    Chesher
    Colin Cuthbert
    Richard Folwell
    A. Gragera/Latin Stock
    B. Murton
    Gregory Ochucki
    Sam Ogden
    Rundi/Tani
    Southampton Oceanogaphy Centre
The Defence Picture Library
U.S. Department of Energy
U.S. Naval Institute
U.S. Navy
U.S. Submarines Inc.
Westland Group
Woods Hole Oceanographic Institution
Lawson Wood/Ocean Eye Films